What Fruit Do You Like?

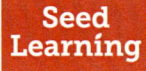

Seed Learning

peaches

oranges

strawberries

grapes

blueberries

kiwis

bananas

watermelons

What fruit do you like?

I like bananas.

What fruit
do you like?

I like strawberries.

What fruit do you like?

I like grapes.

What fruit
do you like?

I like peaches.

What fruit do you like?

I like oranges.

What fruit
do you like?

I like watermelons.

Let's learn about Russia.

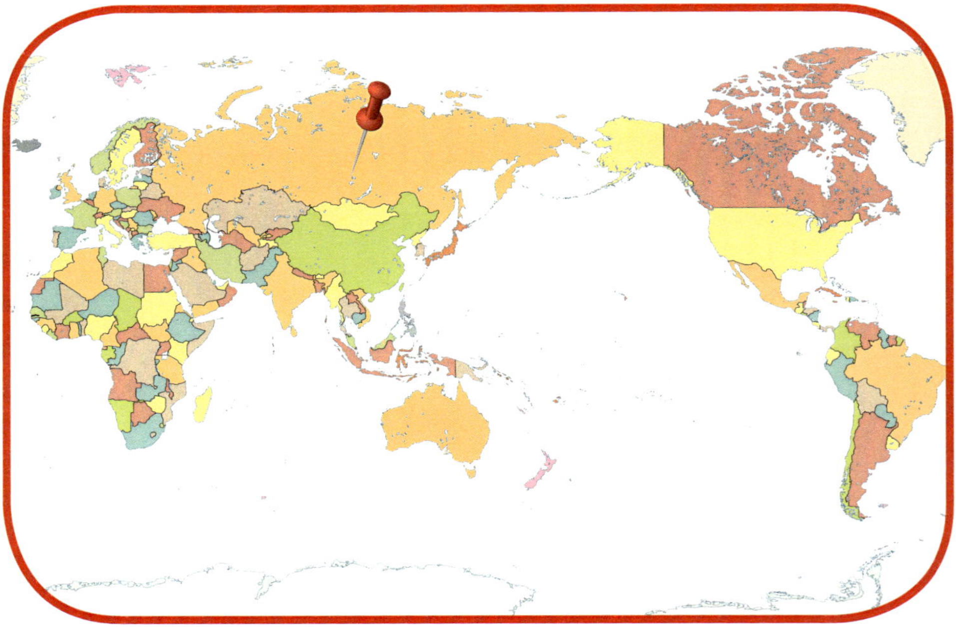

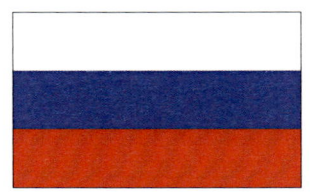

Flag of Russia

Russian nesting dolls